PUFFINS

First published in Great Britain in 1990 by
Colin Baxter Photography Ltd.,
Unit 2/3, Block 6,
Caldwellside Industrial Estate,
LANARK, ML11 6SR

British Library Cataloguing in Publication Data
Dennis, Roy 1940 –
    Puffins.
    I. Puffins
    I. Title
    598.33

ISBN 0-948661-16-X

Photographs by

Front Cover © Dr K Day
Back Cover © Laurie Campbell
Page 19 © K Ghani (NHPA)
Page 20 © Philip Perry (Frank Lane)
Page 21 © N G Blake (Bruce Coleman)
Page 22 © Philip Perry (Frank Lane)
Page 23 © J Watkins (Frank Lane)
Page 24 © Colin Baxter
Page 25 © Tony Wharton (Frank Lane)
Page 26 © Mike Read (Swift)
Page 27 © Philip Perry (Frank Lane)
Page 28 © Paul Taylor (Oxford Scientific Films)
Page 29 © Colin Baxter

Page 30 © Mike Birkhead (Oxford Scientific Films)
Page 35 © Eric & David Hosking
Page 36 © Laurie Campbell (NHPA)
Page 37 © N G Blake (Bruce Coleman)
Page 38 © N G Blake (Bruce Coleman)
Page 39 © Gordon Langsbury (Bruce Coleman)
Page 40 © Colin Baxter
Page 41 © G Ziesler (Bruce Coleman)
Page 42 © G Ziesler (Bruce Coleman)
Page 43 © Colin Baxter
Page 44 © G Ziesler (Bruce Coleman)
Page 45 © M W Powles (Aquila)
Page 46 © Keith Ringland

Puffin illustration © Keith Brockie

Printed in Great Britain by
Frank Peters Printers Ltd., Kendal.

PUFFINS

Roy Dennis

Colin Baxter Photography Ltd., Lanark, Scotland

Puffins

My years at Fair Isle Bird Observatory in the Shetland Islands were made the more memorable by the close presence of Puffins, which lived in the cliffs close by our home. Puffins have a lovely local name in the Shetlands - the Tammy Norrie. Beautiful and brightly coloured among the sea pinks and red campions on the cliffs in May; storm tossed on grey seas below towering black cliffs; comical as they strutted together in their black and white plumage in the evenings; inquisitive as they glided and hovered past me on a bluff in a stiff wind; noisy and quarrelsome as they fought each other down nesting burrows, or angry when I caught them for ringing. Whichever mood, they were always 'Norries' and I remember them as special birds who were my daily neighbours from April to August.

Puffins are members of the Auk family or *Alcidae*. In Britain three other members of this family nest around our shores - namely Guillemot, Razorbill and Black Guillemot. The diminutive Little Auks visit us in winter time from their Arctic nesting grounds and long ago there was the Great Auk which was persecuted to extinction in the 1840's. Elsewhere in the world there are three other members of the Puffin family and they all occur in the North Pacific. The Horned Puffin is most like our bird and is similarly coloured; the main differences are the fleshy protuberances above each eye and a brilliant yellow and red bill. The Tufted Puffin is strikingly different; it is larger and all black with a white face set off by yellow tufts of feathers drooping down from above and behind the eye and curling onto the back, the bill is orange and green, and the legs are orange red. Finally, there is the Rhinocerous Auklet which is about the same size as our Puffin, its upper parts are sooty black and the under parts grey and white, the small bill has peculiar yellow horns pointing upwards near the nostrils and it has white plumes behind the eye and the gape. These three species nest along the west coast of North America, the coast of Alaska and down through the Aleutian Islands to Japan.

Our bird, the Atlantic Puffin, is about 30cm tall and has a wing span of 45cm, it is black above and white below with a white face; the plumage is similar for both male and female. The bill is spectacular. It is brightly coloured and ridged in summer, orange, red, yellow and blue. The eye is brown and surrounded by a bright red ring; above and below the eye are hard pieces of grey skin and behind the eye is a distinct crease in the feathers. The legs and feet are red with black toe-nails. It walks in an upright position, which gives it a Penguin like stance, and it is adept at swimming under water, using its wings half folded. In fact, the wings are small for the size and weight of the bird and this means Puffins have to flap very fast, between 300 and 400 beats a minute, to keep themselves airborne. They are expert at gliding into high winds on the cliffs and manoeuvre using their feet as rudders. In winter they look quite different, the black areas become lighter, the white areas are duller and the face becomes a smoky grey. The horny patches above and below the eye and parts of the bill are shed, to re-grow the following year. At this time of year, Puffins are far out to sea, so they are rarely observed in winter plumage. Occasionally white or albino Puffins are seen, and over the years that I lived on Fair Isle I saw two birds which were mainly white but with some black feathers in the wings and tail. The North Atlantic Puffin is divided into three sub-species, with the population living in the British Isles being the smallest; the birds from further north in Iceland and northern Norway and the Arctic islands are larger, as are the western birds which nest along the coast of Greenland and Canada.

For thousands of years Puffins have lived in the North Atlantic as part of the marine ecosystem, their numbers and distribution have fluctuated, mainly due to climatic effects. During the time of the Ice Ages, Puffins would have nested further south and it is likely that the Puffins now nesting in the Arctic would have been nesting around our shores, and our birds would have been in southern latitudes. As the ice retreated, Puffins, other sea birds and of course the fish on which they feed would have been moved back northwards to the situation that we find today, albeit still influenced by natural cycles.

Man's first influence on Puffins would have been for food and it is likely that they have been eaten from the time that man first started to explore the coasts. With a rapidly increasing human population in the coastal districts of Britain in the 17th, 18th and 19th centuries, large numbers of Puffins were killed for food, especially in places like St Kilda and the outlying islands. The birds were trapped with long handled nets or with hooks and nooses on long poles which could be snagged around the birds' head or feet. The birds were dried or salted, to be eaten either then or later in the season. Puffins have not been regularly eaten in Britain since before the last war and they are now legally protected in our country. Whether the killing and eating of Puffins had any real long term effect on the numbers of birds is open to debate, but as long as the people were not harvesting a greater number than were being produced by the colonies, it is likely that the numbers would have remained relatively stable. Nowadays Puffins are still hunted in this manner in Iceland, where the bird is exceptionally common and they are a regular part of people's diet in the far north.

The number of Puffins breeding in Britain have been the subject of much speculation, and confusion is often caused by descriptions such as "numbers so great they were impossible to count". In 1969, Operation Seafarer organised by the Seabird Group, censussed Puffins along with other seabirds in the British Isles. Those estimates were refined by research organised by Dr Mike Harris of the Institute for Terrestrial Ecology. His estimate of the total British and Irish population was 700,000 pairs of Puffins in 1984 ; 90% of which lived in Scotland, where the majority were in the Outer Hebrides and the Shetlands. The biggest colonies were St Kilda (300,000 pairs), Shiants (77,000 pairs), Foula (70,000 pairs), Hermaness in Shetland (50,000 pairs) and Clo Mor near Cape Wrath (up to 50,000 pairs). About 45,000 pairs breed in Ireland, 20,000 pairs in England and 10,000 pairs in Wales. The world population of North Atlantic Puffins is thought to be 5 million pairs, with the largest numbers in Iceland.

I remember the difficulties in trying to count the numbers of breeding Puffins on Fair Isle when I lived there. The only real way is to count occupied nesting burrows; research in recent decades has established monitoring plots of burrows in various colonies in order to understand Puffin fluctuations. My estimate for Fair Isle in the mid 1960's was 16,000 pairs, but recent and more detailed work suggests 20-30,000 pairs. Part of this may be a genuine increase but it will also be due to more accurate census techniques. We know that Puffin numbers fluctuate in whole colonies and also in different parts of the colonies. In recent decades, colonies on the west side of Britain including St Kilda have declined, many others have remained stable while spectacular increases have occurred in the North Sea. On the Isle of May, off the coast of Fife, Puffins first nested in 1959 with just five pairs, but by 1982 the population had increased to 10,000 pairs!

After spending the winter at sea, Puffins return to land in late March or early April. It was always a special day at Fair Isle when we saw the first Puffins of the year. It was usually on our early morning walk that we first saw them, away across the bay towards the great cliffs of Sheep Rock. Small flocks of black and white birds would swirl around over the sea in the bright morning sunshine. If it was a grey day, then there were just rafts of birds numbering several hundred resting gently on the sea below the cliffs waiting to pluck up courage to come ashore. The date of first arrival in spring is surprisingly uniform and in fact Puffins are very good time keepers. During the time that I studied them at the Fair Isle they always arrived in the last week of March or the first week in April. Twice they arrived in March on the 28th & 30th but more often the date was between the 4th or 7th April. If it was a fine spell of weather the first arrivals would be quickly followed by larger numbers of birds coming ashore all round the island. They take a short time to adjust again to land and then to gain confidence to fly up onto the cliffs to find their traditional nesting sites. At other times if the weather was rough, after a brief visit the birds would disappear to sea for a few days or so until the weather improved. Then they were back in a rush, hundreds and then thousands of Puffins coming back to the cliffs all round the island to reclaim their nesting colonies. Each day, even each hour, they get braver and braver, claiming more and more of their colonies; soon even those with the furthest burrows from the cliff-top are back home. Colonies can be on flat grassy topped islands or cliff tops, grassy slopes, vegetated cliffs and even in crannies and among boulders.

Puffins nest underground unlike their cousins the Razorbills and Guillemots. They excavate a burrow, maybe two metres long, rather like a rabbit burrow and at the end is a nesting chamber where they lay a single white egg. Many of the burrows are used year after year and as long as they return early and have survived the winter, the same pair of

Puffins tend to come back to the same burrow. At other times, a new pair must excavate a fresh burrow in the cliff, usually at the edge of a large colony, or a burrow might have been damaged over the winter and needs to be dug out afresh. Puffins are skilled miners; they have sharp powerful bills which pull at the soil and turf, and the claws on their bright red feet are extremely strong and sharp. One bird goes into the hole and furiously digs, with the earth flying out backwards, propelled by its feet. Quite often its mate stands at the burrow entrance and is showered by flying earth from the burrowing bird. It takes them many days digging to complete a new burrow, so new pairs are keen, if at all possible, to use unoccupied burrows. Puffins often nest near rabbits and sometimes they take over rabbit burrows; that makes life very easy indeed! Puffins are quite able to deal with rabbits, with their sharp bills and pugnacious nature they can easily move a rabbit out of a side burrow.

As burrows are being refurbished or new ones excavated, display among the Puffins increases daily. The pair is together nearly all of the time and between spells of digging, they stand side by side and engage in display. The male is a little bigger and his bill is larger and brighter and more distinctly ridged. The main display is billing and cooing, with the birds touching bills and gently nibbling each other's head and neck feathers. The male may present his mate with bits of vegetation and feathers; at other times they clatter their bills together. This can stimulate nearby Puffins to start displaying or may even provoke an outbreak of fighting which is noisy and at times very bad tempered. A low crooning note is often uttered by the birds, both above and below ground; in fact they have quite a vocabulary of curious moans, groans, growls and crooning. Sometimes pairs fly out to sea in an exaggerated display flight, where they hold their wings high and then beat at half speed. Mating takes place on the sea after the male has gone through a ritual of head flicking and wing fluttering. At times, large numbers of adults perform spectacular massed flights over the nesting colonies; a great continuous circle of flying birds pass over the nesting colony and sweep out to sea in a wheeling motion involving maybe thousands of birds.

The single egg is laid in the nest chamber of the dark burrow, which is often decorated with a few feathers and cliff-top vegetation. It is quite a large, chalky white egg and occasionally has brownish markings. Quickly though, the egg becomes soiled from the bird's feet and feathers as they scurry backwards and forwards in the burrow, changing places during incubation. The egg is incubated by both parents in shifts and they keep it warm with their brood patches on each side of the breast or belly, where naked skin allows close body contact with the egg. Individuals can incubate for over a day, but most incubation stints are shorter than this and the birds change over regularly; some birds even leave the egg unattended for short periods while they fly out to sea. The egg keeps quite warm in its underground nest.

Puffins coming ashore with fish in their bills are the first signs that eggs have begun to hatch. The chick is very small on hatching and is covered with fluffy black down, with a little white down on the belly. The bill, legs and feet are all black. In the early days the small chick is brooded by one of the parents to keep it warm and dry, but soon it can be left unattended so that both parents can go to sea and catch fish. They bring small fish to start, and feed the youngster in the nest chamber, but once the chick is a couple of weeks old it often meets its parents at the mouth of the burrow. They drop the fish on the floor of the burrow and quickly disappear while the youngster feeds. The number of feeds each day varies as the chick grows and reaches a peak of eight to ten feeds a day. When the youngster is about a month old, the feeds start to tail off until the day it fledges. The chicks are quite aggressive, and will fight with other chicks which wander into the wrong burrow. They grow rapidly as long as plenty of food is coming to the nest, and feathers soon start to sprout through the down. By the time the bird is six weeks old it is fully feathered with just a few tufts of down remaining. At this time, the chick comes out of its burrow at night and stands at the entrance in the darkness. Finally, one night when it has reached about seven weeks of age, it leaves its burrow and flies out to sea. By dawn the young Puffin will be well away from land, any of these youngsters that make mistakes at this point are usually killed by gulls or other predators.

During the summer, the attendance by the Puffins at their colonies vary considerably; in fact the daily cycles at Puffin colonies are erratic.

With less fish coming ashore during the middle of the day there are usually more birds at the colony in the mornings and evenings and most of the feeding of the young takes place at these times. The numbers of birds present at the colonies can also vary from day to day, and I remember one spring at Fair Isle counting the numbers of Puffins each evening on a stretch of cliff near my home. Between 27th April and 7th May, at the same place each evening I counted the following numbers of Puffins: 136, 0, 10, 272, 302, 204, 191, 49, 20, 8 and 90. In consequence, it is very difficult to know exactly how many Puffins are living in a particular place and this has always made the counting of Puffin colonies problematic. Puffins can start to nest at three years of age but most of them do not nest until they are four, or more often, five years old, by which time their bills have two distinct ridges and have grown larger. This is essential for the male birds, as the size, colour and character of the bill is one of its most important display features. Often in early summer, younger non-breeding birds visit the colonies and stand around in groups watching the comings and goings of the adults in readiness for the time when they start to breed.

The food of Puffins is fish which they obtain by diving at sea. They catch and eat a range of different species of fish but most often they catch sandeels, sprats and young herring, as well as small whiting and rocklings. One of the more distinctive features of Puffins is their ability to carry numerous fish at one time, often arriving back at the clifftop breeding colonies with rows of small fish held sideways in their bills.

The inside of the upper palate has backward pointing spikes and the tongue has a rough surface. The bird is able to dive into dense shoals of fish and catch one fish after another in the bill, laying each subsequent catch side by side. It is not necessarily true to say that each fish lies head to tail all the way through the bird's bill, it is just chance which way they face, but the bird can carry up to twenty or more small sandeels in its bill at one time. This is valuable from the bird's point of view because it can bring back a good supply of fish for its chick on each journey. It can be dangerous returning to land from these fishing trips, as predators such as gulls and skuas often try to steal the fish that the Puffins bring back.

Most Puffins fish within a few miles or so of their breeding colonies. Puffins and their young depend on a steady supply of food, and if at times the fish stocks fail, especially the sandeels, the chicks become hungry and low in weight, and some of them even die. In very bad years when fish are especially scarce, whole colonies rear only a very few chicks with large numbers of chicks starving to death in their burrows.

Puffins suffer quite a lot of predation, mainly from large birds. It was a common sight in the Puffin colonies that I visited over the years to find the turned-inside-out skins of Puffins littering the ground. Great Black-backed Gulls are the most proficient hunters of Puffins, especially as they manage to catch the birds in flight. They carry the struggling bird to the ground where it is killed; pecking it open they then hold the body and shake it inside out to consume all the edible bits, leaving just the skin, feet, feathers and the hard bill. Great Skuas also catch and kill adult Puffins, while Herring and Lesser Black-backed Gulls take eggs or kill young Puffins as well as being clever at stealing fish from homecoming parents. In some colonies, Peregrine Falcons hunt and kill Puffins while Ravens and Crows take eggs that are laid too near the surface. They will also take young birds if they make the mistake of appearing in the open. Rats and cats can also kill young Puffins.

Arctic Skuas in the Northern Isles are highly skilled at stealing fish from Puffins. They patrol just offshore from the colonies and know exactly which Puffins are returning home with fish. A high speed pursuit takes place as the skua chases a panic stricken Puffin; sometimes the Puffin gets home, sometimes they crash dive below the waves, but often they have to drop their load of fish for the skua and return to sea to try again.

As the summer progresses, Guillemots and Razorbills start to leave the colony, in large numbers in July, the young birds paddling out to sea with their parents. The young Puffins are growing fast in their burrows and non-breeding Puffins start to leave the colonies in August. By mid August nearly all of the Puffins, young and old, have gone. At this time of year, the young Puffin makes an occasional mistake, instead of flying out to sea it crosses land and crashes against a hill dyke or a building or is attracted to a light. When we found birds like this at Fair Isle, which was unusual, we would hold them until the next night, and then take them down to the shore and throw them up into the air to fly away to the ocean. The last stragglers are seen ashore in the latter half of August, and by the end of the month all are gone. A few may still be seen at sea or passing headlands but already the great majority are far from land.

Large numbers of Puffins have been ringed at many sites around the British Isles, but very few of them have actually been recovered away from the nesting colonies. This is due to the fact that Puffins are truly oceanic birds for most of the year. Far more Guillemots and Razorbills are found ashore dead in winter time which is because they winter much closer inshore than Puffins. I ringed many hundreds of Puffins when I lived on Fair Isle; they were exciting days of high summer among the sights and sounds and smells of the huge seabird colonies. Young Puffins were easily ringed as they sheltered in their burrows although I must say it is a dirty exercise as the nesting burrows are not the cleanest of places and there is the added discomfort of Puffin ticks crawling up one's arms! Adults were also caught in burrows; they give very painful pecks with their powerful bills if you make a mistake in holding them. Other adults were caught as they stood at the cliff edge; using a long bamboo pole with a hook at the end, we crawled on our bellies towards them and slipped the hook around their legs. On breezy days, we stood on a high point overlooking the sea and as the Puffins flew inquisitively by, we scooped them out of the air using a long handled net. Occasionally, they were so intent on watching us that they bumped into each other in flight.

Very few of our Puffins were reported away from the island, but occasionally it was interesting to hear of a long distance traveller. One adult I ringed on 10th August 1967 was found dead on the northern coast of Spain on 14th April 1971, while another ringed on 14th July 1969 was found alive on the Isle of May three years later. Mostly our ringing studies provided information on longevity and faithfulness to colonies; our oldest were 23 and 24 years and they were still fit and breeding. Many Puffins from Britain move down through the North Sea to the Bay of Biscay in autumn and occasionally to the Mediterranean. Larger numbers travel through the western coastal waters of Scotland and Ireland, scattering right out across the Atlantic with some reaching Greenland, Newfoundland and even the Canary Islands. Throughout the wild days and nights of winter, our Puffins are out in the stormy Atlantic Ocean far from land, but they are sturdy birds and huge waves are of little concern to them. Surprisingly, it is at this time that the Puffin moults its larger feathers, including its wing feathers and so becomes flightless. As the days lengthen, it regains its powers of flight as well as the brightly coloured sections of the bill, ready for its return to land. At this time, Puffins from Arctic areas come down into the northern Atlantic and the occasional bird which is sick or injured comes ashore and can be identified by its large size.

Puffin wings are relatively small so they flap very fast
(300-400 beats per minute), yet under water
they are small enough to use slightly folded for
diving and pursuing fish. The feet are used as air
brakes in flight and rudders under water.

Home from a winter on the open Atlantic, but not yet ashore.

Small groups come ashore in late March and early April
to claim their nesting burrows. In the beginning they
are hesitant and gather in small parties at the cliff edge,
ready to escape seawards if alarmed.

The huge Puffin colony on the island of Dun, at
St Kilda *(left)*, has been used to study the Puffin's diet.
They are expert fishers. Diving in the open sea, they catch
shoaling fish such as sandeels and their special bills allow
them to securely carry numerous fish back to their young.

Puffins often nest on flower rich sea cliffs, surrounded
by sea campions and thrift. They gather flowers and
vegetation to line their nesting burrows and a large colony
may even destroy much of their attractive surroundings.

Many Puffins now breed on the Isle of May in the
Firth of Forth. It is a small, low offshore island, seen here *(right)*
from the Bass Rock through a cloud of Gannets.

Puffin Conservation

In this century, Puffins have had to face up to many man-made hazards. The first on the scene was oil pollution, as crude and refined oil were shipped across the oceans. When oil is spilt on the sea, the first casualties are sea birds; the oil causes their feathers to become clogged, losing their waterproofing. As well as becoming chilled, the birds try to preen the oil off their feathers and it is ingested and causes serious internal problems. For many decades conservation bodies have strenuously fought to prevent oil pollution at sea. Quite often the matter is made worse by the fact that birds like Puffins, Guillemots and Razorbills seek out patches of oil on the sea because in nature they identify oily patches on the water with fish shoals which are being attacked and eaten by bigger fish under the sea. Actually, Puffins are rarely found oiled, but this is almost certainly due to the fact that Puffins spend most of their year way out to sea. Birds like Guillemots, which more regularly get oiled and come ashore as casualties, winter much closer inshore. It is difficult to say how many Puffins are oiled out in the open ocean and are never reported, but it remains a potential problem, especially near the big breeding colonies in spring or summer. The wreck of the Amoco Cadiz oil tanker off the French coast in March 1978 caused a serious decline in the small population of Puffins along the French Coast.

Other worries for Puffins are the toxic contamination of the seas, and the fish on which they feed. Scientists have identified a variety of different toxic chemicals in Puffins, principally heavy metals and PCB's, but there is no evidence at the present time that this is causing a serious problem for them. Nevertheless it is an underlying worry that these man-made chemicals are present in both the food chain and the Puffin. Even tiny elastic threads and plastics that float on the oceans, by-products of modern society, can be found in Puffin stomachs. Presumably Puffins mistake the elastic threads for tiny fish, but whether they do any serious damage is open to question.

The major problem for Puffins at the present time and for the future is how man exploits the fish stocks of the open seas. Long ago he hunted for big fish, cod and haddock, halibut and skate and the fishing was conducted in a way which did not endanger the resource. But with more and more sophisticated ways of fishing, different species of fish have become scarce and man has moved on to another species. Often this has meant moving down the food chain and in recent decades the catching of sandeels and small fish for the production of fish meal has become a major industry in the North Sea. In the 1970's, Norwegian ornithologists started to find large scale deaths of Puffin chicks on the island of Rost in the Lofoten Islands and studies over a period of years showed that for nearly a decade all of the chicks died while they were still in the burrows. The parents just could not find enough small fish to feed their chicks. During this time there was serious over-fishing of herring, sprats and sandeels along the Norwegian coast. It is believed that there is a direct link between the crash of the fish stocks and the deaths of the Puffins.

In the last 10 years similar situations have started to appear in Scotland, especially in the Shetland Islands. The most obviously affected bird is the Arctic Tern which also feeds on sandeels. Their numbers in Shetland have crashed from 32,000 pairs to 10,000 pairs in ten years, and over the last seven years have not had a single good breeding season. In 1989 less than 100 young were reared from 10,000 pairs of terns! Puffins also feed on sandeels in Shetland and there is real concern that these birds are also being affected by the shortage of small fish. Puffins are more difficult to study than Arctic Terns because they nest underground and in difficult locations, but even so it is believed that 90% of Shetland Puffins failed to raise young in 1989. Clearly this is a major threat to the Puffin.

Sandeel fishing in Shetland started in 1974 and reached a peak of 53,000 tonnes in 1982, since then it has slumped. Ornithologists and conservation bodies expressed growing concern about the over-exploitation of sandeels in Shetland and its effect on seabirds. There was much public disquiet; even some of the fishermen were worried about the removal of fish from the bottom of the food chain. The government was urged to stop sandeel fishing in Shetland but refused because there was considerable argument about whether the shortage of sandeels was really due to overfishing or whether it was due to changes in fish predation by larger fish, or changes in the distribution of sandeels due to changes in climate, ocean currents or plankton. Clearly there was a need for research and after a long delay, during which time research was done on the birds, it became clear that no adequate research was done on the overall ecosystem. However, this matter is now being studied. Nevertheless it would seem prudent while research is done that no further catching of sandeels takes place in these northern waters.

We can't influence the ocean currents or alter the climate quickly or change the fish predators, the only thing we can do quickly is to stop fishing. It is not just to protect Puffins or Arctic Terns but to recognise that these birds are part of a very special ecosystem, and that the Puffin has every right to live along our coasts as we have to exploit the fish in the sea. If we can solve the problems to do with fisheries then the Puffin has a good future, but like so many other birds at the top of the food chain, they will remain a barometer of how well we treat the environment. We must stop polluting the seas, whether it's with crude oil or chemicals or effluents and we must use the marine resources wisely, carefully and self sustainably. If we do all these things, then there is no reason that the Puffins cannot remain a colourful part of our coasts until the next Ice Age.

The Puffin's bill is distinctive, brightly coloured
and attains full size when they reach maturity at four years.
The bill is used in courtship and billing ceremonies *(above)*,
which are frequent in Spring.

Once the eggs are laid and each burrow holds an incubating adult,
the off-duty birds have plenty of time, between feeding trips,
to preen and scratch and meet their neighbours.

Although Puffins usually breed in crowded colonies,
individual pairs nest in crannies and crevices in sheer rock faces.
The high sea cliffs of Foula in the Shetland Isles *(left)*,
provide many such sites.

Mid-summer at Puffin colonies often brings days
of cool sea mists and large numbers of immature birds
emerge – the prospect for future years.

Bright red feet and whirring wings – the fisher home from the sea.

Enjoying Puffins

Puffins are superb birds to watch and to try and photograph. They are easy to identify, but quite often difficult to find without making a special effort.

It is most important to remember to look for them at the right time of year, May and June are the best months, when there is the added bonus that the seacliff flowers are in full bloom and the weather is often sunny and pleasant. Puffins are at the colonies from early April to August; but you can miss seeing them if you are too early or too late in the season. They can also be seen while sea watching from the headlands.

It is best to choose a fine day, without wind and rain, so that it is safer to be on the cliffs. Most Puffin colonies are on or near cliffs, so great care is needed to prevent accidents. Approach Puffins slowly, carefully and quietly; sit and lay down at a distance of 30 metres or so and let them get used to your presence. Closer approaches can be made with care, but do not disturb them too much or prevent them bringing fish to their young later in the season. They are easy birds to photograph but always remember the cliff tops are dangerous. At some localities the Puffins are on islands and it is possible to get good views of them on the water from a boat before landing on the island.

Some of the best sites for seeing Puffins are on outlying islands, such as St Kilda and the Shiants but only small numbers of enthusiasts venture that far; but such visits are unforgettable. Check with bird guides and ask local bird clubs for the best places to see Puffins; the following are some places where Puffins can be observed with varying degrees of ease:

Hermaness, Noss and Sumburgh Head in Shetland

Fair Isle and Foula - both excellent locations for a summer seabird holiday.

Clo Mor and Faraid Head in north west Sutherland.

Dunnet and Duncansby Heads near John O' Groats.

Fowlsheugh, north of Arbroath.

Isle of May, in the Firth of Forth (boat trip).

Farne Islands, off the Northumberland coast (boat trip).

Bempton Cliffs (R.S.P.B. reserve), Humberside.

Portland Bill, Dorset.

Skokholm and Skomer islands in Wales (boat trips).

Puffin Facts

Other Names:

Gaelic - Buthaid   **French** - Macareux Moine

Shetland - Tammy Norrie   **German** - Papageitaucher

Swedish - Lunnefagel   **Dutch** - Papegaaiduiker

Scientific Name: *Fratercula arctica*

Length: 26-29 cms

Bill: 3-4 cms long and deep

Wingspan: 46-63 cms

Weight: Male 400 gms; Female 370 gms; Hatchling 40 gms; Fledgling 300gms. (All measurements are approximate and relate to the average British Puffin)

Average life expectancy of breeding birds: 25 years

Oldest recorded: 29 years

Average annual adult mortality: 5%

Age to first breeding: 5 years, occasionally 4 and rarely 3 years

Races or Sub-species:

Fratercula arctica grabae: British Isles, France, South Norway - smallest

Fratercula arctica arctica: Norway, Russia, Iceland, Canada, West Greenland

Fratercula arctica naumanni: North Greenland, Spitzbergen - biggest

Present on land in UK: from end March to end August

Clutch Size: 1 egg - both adults incubate - single brooded

Egg Size: 61mm x 42 mm - weight fresh 60 gms

Incubation Period: 38-43 days

Fledging Period: 38-44 days

Breeding Population: In Britain 700,000 pairs In world 5 million pairs

Flying Speed: approx 80 km/hr; - wingbeats 300-400/minute

Recommended Reading

The best book for detailed information on Puffins is the excellent monograph, *The Puffin* written by Mike Harris, the acknowledged expert on the species published by T & A Poyser in 1984. A much older book which can be found in libraries and a nice read is *Puffins*, written by R M Lockley and published by Dent in 1953.

Biographical Note

Roy Dennis is a professional ornithologist living near Loch Garten in the Scottish Highlands. For 8 years in the 1960's, he and his wife ran the bird observatory on Fair Isle, famous for bird migration and seabirds. Since then he has worked for the RSPB on Highland birds and their conservation. He has travelled to many countries studying birds, and is a well known lecturer, broadcaster and writer.